An Old Flag

by Tristan Horrom
illustrated by Jennifer Emery

Decodable 16

McGraw Hill Education

Bothell, WA • Chicago, IL • Columbus, OH • New York, NY

MHEonline.com

Send all inquiries to:
McGraw-Hill Education
8787 Orion Place
Columbus, OH 43240

ISBN: 978-0-02-145817-2
MHID: 0-02-145817-0

Printed in China

6 7 8 9 10 DSS 27 26 25 24 23

A home has a big pole.

A boy takes out an old flag.

The flag can go out on the pole.

The boy hopes he can run it up.

He tugs and tugs on a rope.

An old flag waves on a pole!